On the Team

Count to Tell the Number of Objects

Caryl McDonald

ROSEN
MATH
READERS

Rosen
Classroom™

New York

Published in 2014 by The Rosen Publishing Group, Inc.
29 East 21st Street, New York, NY 10010

Book Design: Katelyn Londino

Photo Credits: Cover, pp. 5, 13, 16 (team) Comstock/Thinkstock.com; pp. 7, 16 (player) Stockbyte/Thinkstock.com;
p. 9 © iStockphoto.com/kali9; p. 11 iStockphoto/Thinkstock.com; p. 15 Digital Media Pro/Shutterstock.com.

ISBN: 978-1-4777-1584-0
6-pack ISBN: 978-1-4777-1585-7

Manufactured in the United States of America

CPSIA Compliance Information: Batch #CS13RC: For further information contact Rosen Publishing, New York, New York at 1-800-237-9932.

Word Count: 25

Contents

The team has 5 players.

Matt is player 1.

Kayla is player 2.

Nate is player 3.

Sasha is player 4.

Drew is player 5.

Words to Know

player

team

Index